DOMINIQUE HECQ

OTOPOS

DOMINIQUE HECQ

OTOPOS

Published by Beltway Editions, 4810 Mercury Drive, Rockville, Maryland 20853.

www.beltwayeditions.com

Printed in the United States of America
10 9 8 7 6 5 4 3 2 1

Book Design: Jorge Ureta Sandoval
Author Photo: Michael Reynolds
ISBN: 978-1-957372-14-3

Beltway Editions (www.beltwayeditions.com)
4810 Mercury Drive
Rockville, MD 20853
Indran Amirthanayagam: Publisher
Sara Cahill Marron: Publisher

A person is a community of beings,
an 'us' as much as an 'I'
—Jane Hirshfield

Contents

PREFACE

Otopos unfurls a paradox: the interleaving and entangling of self and topos. It began with a loss of equilibrium impelling rhythmic departures, an incipient blood beat—subcutaneous, through the feet all the way to the surface of the page. A Belgian native, I live and write on unceded Wurundjeri land in an inner-city suburb of Melbourne. This makes me a paradox. An unsettled European out of place in a neighbourhood she calls home with its fenced, stolen and, too often, desecrated land. Who bears witness to political abstractions and aberrations yet fails to wholly reimagine or rematerialize these through poetry despite her attempt to uncover the regimes of terror of settlement perpetrated by the symbolic. Whose breath catches again and again.

Otopos is a reckoning, an elegy, an ode to the Merri Creek trail that snakes through Melbourne's northern suburbs and colluvial slopes, teaming with native flora and fauna, but also imported weeds and predators, including humans. In its arrangement in three parts, the collection unfolds displaced fragments and glimpses of histories through call and response of landscapes and beings. The poetics active here is a poetics of the liminal: from word to word, line to line, space to space the narrative persona writes its shoreless existence, roaming as it does through lexicons and topographies.

****

OTOPOS

****

1.

Lulled by the night's lingering breath, the city hibernates. Funnelling wind at your back, you skirt the creek. Follow the trickle of bruises the light leaves in its wake. You take the path down to the bridge, the no-sun enfolded in fog. Eucalypts rustle. Reeds rumour. Australian wood ducks, chestnut teals and a lone hardhead on corrugated water. Magpie larks chatter in a she-oak. A nankeen night heron darts in your path as if to say you don't exist. Under the bridge, a black swan on a nest intermeshed with plastic. Now the wind embraces you. Mud sucks at your boots—*ssk ssk ssk*. Rainbow lorikeets, fairy corellas and musk lorikeets clatter about. You climb the escarpment. Here, creeping bent grass, English broom, arum lily, prickly pear, periwinkle overflow garden fences. Gusts of wind through veils of bridal creeper and poison ivy.

2.

Walk with me, says the voice drowning in its own rasping sound. You become it, the voice, a shapeshifter like the creek itself, brimming with unspoken thoughts, voiceless bubbles, breathless refuse.

Waterfall. Murky calm where the path tilts and narrows.

Here, the water curves and swerves in its own bed, pulls at silt. The current pushes it out unseen, against the sunken stepping stones.

Here, the water swirls, froths, falls and rushes towards the edge land of daydream. Towards the immargination of the page.

3.

A wattlebird babbles on the other side of the window. I replenish the water bowl. Spot a honey eater hopping about in the fuchsia.

My hand yawns. It is a beak opening.

Water breaking at the touch of a feather.

I am a magpie. Warble a wattlebird prattle.

I feel for the shape of a poem.

I live and work on the land of the Wurundjeri people of the Kulin Nation, the sovereignty of which was never ceded. I acknowledge its traditional custodians, offering respect and gratitude to their ancestors, elders and families past, present and in perpetuity.

Australia always was and always will be, Aboriginal land.

I feel shame, not quite guilt, for knowing so little about the languages, cultures, and customs of the Kulin Nation. For purloining the bird's call. For naming it prattle.

(*To unwrite the I from the poem. Think of it*).

4.

Words are possums crawling up the walls of silence. They have razor-sharp claws. They pounce. They can see in the dark. They will poke the apple of your eye. Hook your mouth shut. Rip you to shreds. Tear up your dreams one letter at a time.

Pause.

Consider the damage to the root of your tongue.

Don't worry: they will burst the blisters tenderly. At dawn they'll scuttle around the idea of noise. Then they will burrow under the vault of your ribs and nibble at the chambers of your heart.

Here, they will persuade you to shrug off your graphomania, glossolalia, xenolalia. Tendency to anaphora and… apocrypha.

5.

Cold bites, breath dissipates
gossamer mist nudges the windowpane.

Sky low over Melbourne.

The sun wears a corona of grey that keeps it away
from the day
like a foreign body's swathing
so intimate it blinds.

I fumble for the shape of a poem.

Pelting rain. The wind dies. Ink spills.

This is how the I unwrites itself from the poem.

The sky won't fall for all its broken lights.

Waves of wheeling spectral spokes follow
you like a sailing dream.

Open the window.

Float past your life.

You could go along a straight line for light years;
the angle at which you'd see sun and moon
and shade and sea would be the same.

This is how you unwrite yourself from the poem.

A boat loaded with broken mirrors sets alight
memories of a past for live masks.

A boat loaded with dry brambles lights nightmares
of a present for death faces.

A boat loaded with paper aeroplanes matches
dreams of a future for unborn forms.

On the nearby shore, ash of us in shimmering shadows.

6.

Another lockdown. Your pen interrupts
itself half-way through a line. You hug
the sky. Come out of hiding.

The lounge is littered with photo paper,
twine, sticky tape, a notebook, bubble
wrap and four phallic sculptures lying
on their sides.

The kitchen is a tapestry
of left-overs on plates that don't match.

The bedrooms are full of humans, their
avatars, screens and keyboards.

Lambent light beckons. You steal
out of the house in search of a poem.

Skitter down to the creek, anti-clockwise.
Climb the rocky escarpment
past the rickety bridge.

Bees and honey eaters in fire sprite grevilleas.
Dogs and people everywhere. Wattle
in the air. Sound of a bagpipe.

You cut across the wetlands. Survey
the plants: tussock grass, paper
daisies, spear-grass, everlastings,
orchids, lilies, periwinkles, maidenhair.

Your heart leaps at the sight of the scarlet
runner, and the word turns where it means to go.

7.

I've never counted the bones in my hand, but I have an extra finger shaped like a honey eater's beak—an esoteric bit of fleshed out bone that blocks all light except the liquid bandwidth emitted by ionised hydrogen in burning honey that reveals the cloying structures of gas corralled by magnetic fields and birds of paradise.

My extra finger enables me to feel the inside of blackwood buds. Taste the nectar of their nebulae-filled umbraphile flowers. Smell the heat of what will be called this year's hydrogen alpha bee bushfire. See the next total eclipse of the sun at Exmouth. Capture the cosmic inferno that will be known in one thousand and one nights. The mother of utter silence.

8.

Tugging tang of night.

Swell of sounds: currawongs call, lorikeets shriek, magpies intone a toccata.

Daybreak unfurls its curtain of light. Sunshine turns away from your window.

Quarantined, you become a nomad. You walk towards the edge of the civilised world. Set yourself apart. Look for the real on the edge of insanity. Inanity. With every pace, the weight of your body shifts. There is nothing solid underfoot. You try chassés with and without port de bras. A leap. Legs tremble. Find balance. Your feet pick up the dance. Ascend wordless climes. You climb down.

When night falls and you come back in your body, the house will dissolve and run as the virus roves across the globe.

9.

Watching the wind ruffle the leaves outside our bedroom window, birdsong like I've never heard before in Melbourne. I can even hear bell birds pinging from the creek. Golden light. Odour of lilac. I hope we can retain this new skill of mindful appreciation.

Now I understand why in *Tirra Lirra by the River* the protagonist's first sexual experiences are set among cherry laurels: pungent smell of honey.

Mid-walk, the skies open. Rain pours. Yellow water rises, swirling about, soon gushing out of the creek's banks, carving furrows among grass, reeds, bushes and trees. The dog takes the lead and pins us to the bridge.

Murky calm where the path tilts and narrows.

Here, the water curves and swerves in its own bed, pulls at silt. The current pushes it out unseen, against the sunken stepping stones.

Here, the water swirls, froths, falls and rushes towards the edge land of daydream. Towards the immargination of the page.

(*Unwrite the I from the poem*).

10.

zero time moonless dark.

i should have hurtled after you in spite
of the curfew but instead recomposed my alphabet.

were you to return from this too long
an impulse i'd tell you to sit with me.

i'd tell you to listen.

look, we are not hermits.

11.

anatomists of love atomise agape into ablated symbols of absence
babies are born breathing with the unbearable burden of being
chromosomes come in pairs (ex)cruciating the stars
distancing describes the disjunction death demands of us
epitaphios is the most heartrending elegy a mother ever conceived
fontanelles are an infant's soft spots prefiguring mellifluous kisses
grey griffins grip time's edges as generic memory turns to gold
hearing hastens amygdala and hippocampus hip hop
i cling to the idea that ideation need not kill i with id
joy animates itself like a jaguar in the jungle
kulik invokes *flashbulb memory* to speak of quirky panic attacks
language is a labyrinth layered with flesh and soul
metamorphic museums exhibit the mind's minute mirrors
neurasthenics negate the oneiric neverland they navigate
once you broke your odyssey and i promised you an origami orchestrion organ
perhaps the painterly poetry pluming my veins poisoned you
quaint qwertyuiop letters pick a quarrel in the quince tree
recollection means ripping reverie remnants from intranquillity
screen memories scrape the surface of the symbolic
tympani are the typhoons of titillated hearts

unconscious associations usher us towards unsounded universes
voices evade vision the way vixens veer off vinyl grooves in *Vatic Evolution*
wrangling with words wakes a whirlpool of waxwings
xeres quixotic on my breath i hear a xylophone tick a tix a tick ticking
your life is no yoke yodelling yeti lexis yoyo but a yearning
zigzags zip zap zizz asterisks buzz zygotes fuzz in febrile zephyr

12.

and here you are all pallor sick with lockdown brittle as
a ghost succumbing

to the malady of the cosmos eyes shucking shadows but
i don't
need to tell you that.

sit with me

(   )

listen

(   )

we are not hermits

(   )

unmasked and agile again you wander down the creek as
i close

unseeing eyes on dawn's flamingo flamboyance

praying for a reprieve.

13.

Look. Listen.

Tell me if you catch sight of the spotted pardalote. She is tiny. Forages for insects in the leaves of gum trees. I've never seen her—*dedee dedee dedee dedee*, she calls.

Tell me if you catch sight of the dancing willie wagtail and the superb fairy-wren.

Tell me if you catch sight of the dark-olive green whipbird—*whip whip whip whip.*

Tell me if you catch sight of the silver bird who crossed our path only two days ago.

Tell me if it's an egret.

Does it matter?

Listen.

14.

Lulled by the night's lingering breath, the city hibernates. Sucking wind at your face, you skirt the creek. Follow the trickle of bruises the light leaves in its wake. You take the path down to the bridge, the no-sun enfolded in fog.

Here, creeping bent grass, English broom, arum lily, prickly pear, periwinkle overflow garden fences. Gusts of wind through veils of bridal creeper and poison ivy.

Eucalypts rustle. Reeds rumour. Myas and blackbirds and crested pigeons patrol the wetland. Under the bridge, a water-loving hen, head jerking, goes *kerk kerk kerk*. Two tawny frogmouths huddle in a gum tree. Magpie larks swoop—*peewee peewee peewee.*

You hobble on the bridge. Swing to the right. A bell pings. You skip left to avoid the lycra cyclist.

At the playground, a red-headed, white-cheeked rosella, legs encased in ash. Her upper breast is crimson, lower breast lemon fading to pastel green. The feathers on her back and shoulders are black with yellowish margins scalloping away towards a rainbow tail. Her beak is mother of pearl. You hold your breath.

15.

Walk with me, says the voice rising in its own whistling sound. You become it, the voice, a shapeshifter like the creek itself, brimming with unspoken thoughts, voiceless bubbles, breathless refuse.

Waterfall. Murky calm where the path tilts and narrows.

Here, the water curves and swerves in its own bed, pulls at silt. The current pushes it out unseen, against the sunken stepping stones.

Here, the water swirls, froths, falls and rushes towards the edge land of daydream. Towards the immargination of the page.

(*Unwrite the I from the poem*).

16.

The day without ceremony begins with blackbirds Bells unhinged Silence is an air bubble breaking I move amid feathers beneath unbuttoned eyes Light Unmusical yet rhythmical sounds echo in the room Voyce, face closed, touches the stigmata of language Silence is an air bubble breaking, I say A quizzical expression beclouds her face Laughter bursts in her voice I touch the sky Phonemes cut the air Images, words, letters cascade Tropisms rustle inside Voyce and I, one and the other conjoined in the obsolete art of conversing Call it a wave of sound Tide of noise Unmusical yet rhythmical A horn blast Funny how the world seeps through the conversation Cracks meaning Sorry, that's not what I meant at all Images, words, letters cascade. Litter the floor (the forward movement of speech is associative rhythm connection disconnection repetition disconnection disrupted flux *tending-not-tending-to-hemiola*) Tropisms rustle inside Voyce and I, one and the other conjoined in this disappearing life We trail off into silence I can be played on any instrument I, or Voyce, then says *Shh Shh Shh* Did you **hear**? A kind of hum A high and eerie keening Voyce is not a person of many words Her face closed, she touches the stigmata of language before language A fractal fugue floats through the air I gesture towards the piano Puffing exhalations, chiming, puffing exhalations Voyce sits down at the instrument Rip tide of sound I am speechless *one*-**and**, *two*-**and**, *three*-**and**, *four*-**and**, *five*-**and**, *six*-**and** Her hands move so swiftly and fluidly on the keyboard of language before the stigmata of language it's hypnotic Black birds white birds black fish white fish black frogs white frogs black birds And winding up the performance *one-***and**, *two-***and**, *three-***and**, *four-***and**, *five-***and**, *six-***and** *seven-***and** Voyce finishes with a parodic flourish Wow! *Clap Clap Clap* We glide inward toward the very centre of Escher's Verbum.

****

THE MERRI CREEK MURDERS

****

Yesterday, I thought I saw a bird
But there are all kinds of quick shadows now
—Joan Fleming

1.

You call us river gums. We don't mind. We're all family, though your botanists call us different names—swamp gum, red box, red stringybark, manna gum, grey box, yellow box. Even the she-oaks don't mind your botanists' names. Those names are pretty literal. We hope they remind you we just are. We sway and creak in the wind. This doesn't mean we don't feel, hear, see. We do. We see further than you.

Today the story begins with a human jogging along the Merri Creek. We don't give you names, assign you a species, genus or gender. They're oblivious to the whipping of their ponytail on their cheekbones. They are oblivious to the amber baubles of bitter kangaroo apples. They stomp past step after step as they loop their way back under the bridge. They're thinking about gyrfalcons. How they fly out and always return, even when the leash breaks. We snicker at the fantasy. But we shouldn't. The eutaxia and honey pots shiver. Huddle and droop from sight. We sway and creak. Know better than to say aloud their ponytail drags them back to the nearby bushes. We smell leather, the pale hood falling over her eyes. Yes, we know they are a young woman. It's an old story. We smell fear and leather and blood. We see her assailant. He takes her through her skin thin bark.

A sound like the cry of the tawny frogmouth in the dead of night. But it is dusk, and already the haunting begins. A helicopter hovers over the wetlands. Our whispers cut to the quick. Our ears flap shut. You'll hear the whirring and buzzing and droning through the night. You will toss and turn, imagining the young woman's whereabouts. You'll get up and dress in the dark. Then you will lace up your running shoes. And run. Don't plug your ears. Watch out for us. We see what you can't see. We record what you call the invisible. Our fibres are feelers growing thick with rumours.

2.

It could have been me. I was in her stride. Smelled her fear as the air shook. Took a call. Dialled 000. Laid down my heart.

She may have heard them, the footsteps. Snipping twigs, crackling leaves. Her phone hummed its Pegasus tune, a premonition, I imagined. It burrowed into her ears with the same persistence as a tapeworm. She wished it trapped inside her earbuds. Yanked them off and threw them onto the track.

I raced back along the curvilinear creek. Looped back under the bridge, over it past the cricket ground. Watched from the other bank, voiceless, head throbbing, unsure what to do.

It could have been me. Could have been you.

3.

Hands clipping the native currant bush, I looked on.

He pushed her, dragged her into the nearby bushes and unzipped. He kicked her, hit her again, said lucky he's not throwing her into the creek and then he did. He jumped into the water. Hit her face with an open hand, then with a closed fist and choked and choked. He asked, Do you like that you bitch? And she fought back like crazy pulling his hair, packing a punch. And he laughed like crazy, hit her again and choked her and pushed her head under, said how lucky no one's looking.

No tear no scream no voice

untracked unknown unheard un

t i l

( )

4.

The girl leapt out of the blue
where the track narrowed across from the stepping
stones below the dam youngsters built last summer.

I pulled the dog off her path.
We skipped aside to let her through.

Early twenties. Black tights. White T-shirt.
Hair tied in a purple band. Ears plugged.

The kids cracked up at her aviator sunnies.
I smoothed their heads. We pushed on.

An ordinary afternoon: Air sparkling, people everywhere.
Frogmouths huddling high up in the trees. Ibises cruising
through the sky. Dogs wading in the creek, din of bellbirds.

Time suddenly adrift.

5.

We smelled that fear, that leather, the blood. We saw her assailant. How he took her through her skin thin bark.

Crows *kraah kraaah.* Stick insects scratch. The haunting has begun. A helicopter over the wetlands. Our whispers cut to the quick. Our ears flap shut.

Whirring, buzzing, droning through the night. Toss and turn, you imagine the woman's whereabouts. You already know the psychologist will fail to take action. The only witness will refuse to testify. The rapist will get off lightly.

Next morning, you'll not listen to the news. You'll get up, dress in the dark. You'll lace your running shoes. And run.

Don't plug your ears. Watch out for us. We see what you can't see. Record what you call the invisible. Our fibres are feelers growing thick with rumours.

Perpetually the earth catches death flowing along the creek or tangled in the wafting reeds or shaking itself loose from our grizzling limbs.

6.

Red sun sinking in your backyard. She blots out the choking, the near drowning. Slips the knots of her shoelaces, slides out her legs to relieve her tight chest and scuffs the back of each running shoe across the kerb till first her heels then her toes are free. She belly-crawls, finds her knees, hoists herself up against a rubbish bin. It stinks of rotting fish.

Her hands throb, but the tune in her earphones has gone. And with it, the fear.

You are still looking, do
nothing.

Listen.

No tear no scream no voice

untracked unknown unheard un

t i l

the next blow.

7.

Light at the end of the path as he turned into the gateway and from the yard gushed words like it would be nice to have something cold to drink.

But in the dark corner near the shed where the linden tree shook its leaves and showered pollen were slivers of pale flesh cleaved off by the sheer radiance of jouissance.

A cold gust of wind.

He lifted his weight forward into the long grass, dug his boots in the soft soil, step slow yet erratic, fist closed on the knife.

He stopped.

I retched.

8.

I clapped eyes on the shape of a woman tearing through the trail. She did look ahead. Even tried out a smile. Said hello to middle-aged women who crossed her path, scooping up their dog's shit in black bags. I bet she felt ripped in half. Wracked, surely. She may have considered the disarray of her own life as you'd say in your artsy lingo.

But she pushed on, pumping her calf muscles. She stepped over crack after crack on the footpath as her feet stumbled forward catching dirt, leaves, shit and gravel. She turned right, which felt wrong as the sun bit her back and hacked at the shape of her life.

It has no outline now, her life. It resembles a twig, or is it a thorn. It catches her spangled tights. A hole. A rip that slowly undoes the fabric.

Now that having vanished, you'd say, she has become an abstraction.

The idea of a woman at high velocity.

9.

You call us River Gums. We don't mind. We watch and listen with the silence slinking through our limbs and boughs under the glare of the knowing sun, gaze of the knowing moon. We know things, too. But we are not psychics. Our fibres are feelers growing thick with rumours not omens. And we remember. We remember the year of your lord 1936 with the silence slinking through our limbs under the glare of the knowing sun.

Having pleaded guilty to having conspired with Violet Ada Walker (23) of East Brunswick to murder her and himself, Edward Miller (39), of North Fitzroy, was sentenced to nine months gaol. Miss Walker was found dead on the bank of Merri Creek on January the 7th and the evidence given at Miller's trial was that he and Miss Walker agreed to commit suicide... Justice Duffy said It had been urged on the prisoner's behalf that a prosecution of this kind was without precedent. His Honour assumed in the prisoner's favour…

Today our thoughts turn to a woman's pummelled torso found among rushes bull and black.

10.

name's rick carson
them call me spikes
druids' captain.

oi seen him man he knuckled & kicked & knuckled & kicked that sheila / he just went on & on & then he tripped her & knocked her hard on the head & he shagged her o man / oi kouldna bleevit in & out in & out in & out he just went on & on / effin reckless & then he threw her in the creek & jumped in & pushed her head under & choked her & pushed & choked / he just went on & on upter & me oi got struck dumb / with fear for her o man 't was orrible orrible & oi did nothin & oi told no un / but aorto do somethin ardunno .

so why dinoi speak up mayte?

oi'm speakin up now cos aorto do something.

NOW.

11.

A man who can't be named for legal reasons allegedly attacked a female jogger late yesterday afternoon. He allegedly raped her numerous times and threw her in the water. He allegedly held the woman's head under water during the assault, which placed her in danger of death. He allegedly repeatedly strangled her. The woman allegedly managed to free herself and walked to a side street off the Merri Creek trail hoping to get help but her attacker allegedly caught up with her. Other details of the alleged attack are too graphic for release to the public.

We have established a crime scene. Our members are scouring the waterways and bushlands for clues, or possible remains. Detectives from the Sexual Crimes Squad are now appealing for information from anyone who witnessed the incident. The alleged offender is in custody and there is no further threat to the community in relation to this incident. Police have increased patrols around the creek and surrounding parklands. They would like to reassure the community they can continue to live their lives and go about their daily business—as is their right to do so safely. A local resident who runs along the trail with a group of women said they were planning a march called *Reclaim our Merri Creek* for Sunday evening. The group will meet at Mayer Park at 6 pm.

12.

We of the Merri Merri know it's harder to read than see, hear, feel, for we have seen it all—the infanticides, matricides and parricides, the senseless and maniacal crimes. We've seen it all, heard it all, felt it all—lust, desire, rage, wrath, fury, hatred, obsession, cruelty, callousness and ignorance. See where the path forks, just off the rickety footbridge?

We thought the jogger would make it to what you call Harding Street.

Turned out different.

We call that a fluke of fate.

There'll be the smarting delay of closure after the march, the vigil, the mass of flowers mounting on the banks of the creek with the red sun sinking. There'll be tears and screams and hushed voices. Then silence. The smell of rotting blooms and silt and dust as you carry on with your jogging and cricketing and footy training and kite flying and dog walking among your children laughing.

But we'll remember.

13.

Night, laced with mist

a slight quiver of breeze, oblivious

to the internal weather of your heart

you watch your brilliant window recast
in a full reflection the white linen curtains billowing
gently

Here, *heeere*, calls a currawong, and you are back at the water's edge, watching
a plastic bag bobbing along the creek, or some severed head smooth as the moon

You taste the bitter taste of juniper, inhale the damp
reek of a body cleaved from a bed of reeds and roots,
all tangled

Nothing holds it now, the body. It balloons downstream,
leaving you unleaving

Sweat on your thinning skin evaporates, or is it silt
dusting its translucence as your Dante holds vigil
at the sinking moon, and you sur/face

You forget where you are; everything is

cold to the touch

wavelets unfold before you, voice a trickle of white ink.

FERVOUR

Falling in love
is glamorous hell; the crouched, parched heart
like a tiger ready to kill
—Carol Ann Duffy

1.

At the Sacred Kingfisher Festival we danced to the beating of drums, our laughter rapturous and rebellious among the pinging of bellbirds. The air smelled of river mint wild myrtle and boronia as a red haze rose between us and the horizon line. In the bog garden we chased the wandering sun and you picked golden billy buttons and we kissed under the tessellated tower of my hair. Caped in your fake lion skin you said I reminded you of Castilla. Who is she, I asked in an intermixing of levity and seriousness. We ate steamed mussels and fried calamari, olives and hot peppers, octopus *a feira* and gazpacho. We drank tequila. Liked its hot spring in our bellies. We sucked on lemons and ice. Already my heart felt unparched, its chambers soft inside its suckering pericardium. You blew through the bushes and wetland bullrushes without a word like a bird or the wind itself.

Was it love's fervency and desire we had interlaced,
together?

2.

I seek you everywhere through the grasslands and woodlands and shrublands. Through spiny headed mat rushes tufted bluebells sickle ferns and pussy tails. I tear trough spear grass and around patches of golden wattle silver banksia and swamp paperbark. At the curve in the creek where the river red gum stands I cut a heart out of its bark for a shield. The gum bleeds but I lash through wedge leaf hop bushes and rosemary grevilleas slashing punctuation save the arrhythmical lone period. For now.

I seek you in shoals of fish.

I seek you in clouds of bats.

I seek you in schoolings of tadpoles.

I seek you in murders of crows.

I seek you in the sturdiness of your name

I seek you in the word *lover.*

3.

I find you in music and painting and poetry. I find you in myth and make you mine. Kneading words as one would dough beyond the trammels of the self where reminiscences and expectations deflate being and slowly I rise from its shell shaping what beckons like a promise.

I surrender to the sky like a flowering gum deploying its satin.

I reach for your hand and touch only a dream blossoming spikes.

Slowly. I rise from emptiness. Shaping what becomes a prayer.

You wave to me from outside the gleaming window when out of the blue a little kingfisher flies into the glass.

Look how stunned the bird is. How it shakes itself off from shadow sheen. And flies away.

4.

Sacrifices ensure rebirth. So do libations and other ceremonies of purification for animals at play in the arena of language.

I call you my significant other.

The question is are you worth
losing all, even
my children?

For you know I am married
though I discard the adverb men use
like a self-fulfilling prophecy—
yes, that one: happily.

I pledge to choose

my words more carefully.

5.

A drooping she-oak with fissured bark and wiry branchlets needles neglect.

In the distance a flock of cockatoos keen like a cascade cascading.

My husband's booming voice abolishes music as readily as his bulbous eyes obscure my shadow.

A fierce northerly blows to shreds the velvety leaves of the peppermint geranium.

I rein in a poem as though cadences could eradicate murderous fantasies.

Writing witnesses that which yearns and yawns.

6.

Consorted!

It rained rice on the congregation like aerodynamic grief.

This is a long time ago – when
I had not yet realised
marriage sealed by pity or perhaps even charity
comes with wax so cold it hardens love – so
called.

No. I didn't know yes
could kill.

The story goes I was bequeathed worship fast as a bullet more hypothetical than real perhaps as neither images nor similes nor symbols nor metaphors do signify.

7.

Then at the bend of t*he river of mists and shadows the wind of uncertainty blew at the peak of acquired knowledge*, your teal gaze daring the baring of bows and arrows at the Rising festival, though it was fall.

Kangaroo apples were out and the soles of our feet, toughened by seasons of walking barefoot, took us to the ghost *yorra yorra* and millennial waters cascaded upon our backs and we took a boat at nightfall and disrobed further up Country where waters were once sky blue and we watched the radiant moon grow into a blood drop against a jet-black sky enfolding lines of flight.

We parted at the bend of the river of mists and shadows, listening to the voice of the land and baby leaf eels caught in a sliver of brightness singing *iuk iuk iuk iuk* in a language we didn't

8.

KNOW

how our lengthening shadows would
surrender to the purpling sky
like a secret secret straining

open

as if one intake of breath could inverse

the order of things out there where there is no time but a heartbeat.

Light lashes the limbs of blackwoods.

Honey eaters hover

over silver banksias bursting with nectar.

In the pond tiny frogs *croak croakle croak*.

9.

How unstill everything is.

Too many words swarm before the idea of the real, the imaginary always shimmering out of reach.

The mathematical sublime against dynamic sublimity *which brings about what nature could not finish.*

We live existence among black metal albums already tarnished with ash because *what is excessive for the imagination is... an abyss, in which it fears to lose itself.*

Life is a chromatic fractal slipping into dusk.

Love is a rainbow whose colours vanish after downpour.

10.

Real and hypothetical children I loved beyond the confines
of being with the unsuspecting
powers of the heart, clawing
at the air when water already tasted of algae blooming
absence.

To forget the commotion of the universe, time
and time again I wrote to bear
witness to that which yearns and yawns and sometimes
yields.

The replication of fervour and failure.

The sacrifices enacted to ensure the return of the wandering sons.

The ravishing of Cybele in the Anthropocene.

Grief is a currawong's call in the dead of night.

11.

And here you are, the wind at your back, a red flag
fluttering on the horizon line, or is it the valley quietly
afire just before smoke curls and rises and sparks crackle
and crack, crawling up the limbs of trees like commas
creep, licking the back of this poem.

The question is,
is it worth losing all, even
my children?

I let it flutter, the word love
now that the wind bends back, bringing the far closer
and further afar now that I pin you down on the page
among the tufted bluebells and pincushions and scarlet
runners where red is redder than blood and green
greener against red where our bodies fail to hear the
music rise where the river sings *iuk iuk iuk iuk iuk*.

12.

No, I didn't realise that yes
could kill.

My marriage resembles Husserl's *époché.*

The negative move whereby I bracketed out the world.

[not a step I took to brace myself for reduction proper]

No, the bracketing and the move whereby I drove my self back upon its very self, crushing it as it crashed through glass.

[ ]: a contrafactual phenomenon, an error of perception, linguistic transcription and interpretation with a body drawn to the dead beat of silence failing to hear the percussive music of the heart.

13.

Heart unparched, its chambers soft inside its suckering bark.

You blow through the bushes and the wetland's bullrushes without a word like a bird or the wind itself.

After rain at dusk, oblivious to clouds frowning past Mercury.

A flash of blue as tiny and brief as light reflecting off a raindrop.

The prodigal sun reaches out for a hand.

To brush off all errors of perception, transcription, interpretation.

To love till love is but a word of recall.

14.

A million groggy wee leaf eels burst through storm drains
wave in brown water through green rushes
scattering like momentous though impossible
hope: the un
said un sayable
music of the heart our bodies strive to but can't

hear as gorges swell and waters cascade through
impossible hope and the page turns
to silt river

ominous like a dream

my face obscured by your radiance.

Possessed with magic at *yorro yorro* I course through the moonlit landscape to where the world calls for reversals and *amid the glow of day break.*

I summon your name, *deark* dear K.

15.

When I wake, I see not the sky's artistry shooting through time in a swarm of equinoctial colours pinking the dawn, but your radiant face, eyelids enfolding teal eyes and twilight, your body moored to the edge of aquamarine, turquoise, peacock blue.

Taste, smell, hear, touch the air looping and whirling desire drowning the night.

Heartbeat, a swell between us
after a long-held breath.

Blueberries, aniseed, patchouli, emerald blue spangles
between water and sky
seagulls pecking meringue clouds
the bridge between us dissolving.

16.

I forget I am coming
to, kneading rock into Eros
shapes on the shore.

O deark dear K *amid the glow of day break*
forehead a blank page I name *aqua profonda.*

And, yes!

I rise from Botticelli's shell as you scallop words
like lip, ear, wing and brush
philtrum, columella, cantus in the misting mist.

The air seems to grow violets and you gather their heart leaves.

NOTES

Otopos

The epigraph is an excerpt from an essay on the relationship between poetry and the factual simply titled 'Rabbit Homework' by Jane Hirshfield published in *Rabbit*, a journal of nonfiction poetry (vol. 31, 2020).

Stanza 6 alludes to *Tirra Lirra* by the River, a novel by Australian author Jessica Anderson (Penguin, 1978).

'Epitaphios' (stanza 11) references an elegy Australian writer Beverley Farmer wrote in memory of a child she lost at Easter 1975. It features in *A Body of Water* (UQP, 1990). Farmer would no doubt have known *Επιτάφιος*, Yannis Ritsos's poem about a mother losing an adult son in the 1936 strike of Thessaloniki tobacco workers.

Cognitive psychologists Roger Brown and James Kulik coined the term 'flashbulb memory' to designate a shocking event that preserves the lived experience of it.

Vatic Evolution is a paratext by Virginia van Vreemd (Vivid Press, 2021).

Stanza 16, originally called, 'Anaphora' took its title from Elizabeth Bishop's poem of the same name. The opening line echoes Bishop's first two lines. I wanted to contrast speech and music because it seems to me that the associative rhythm of music mimics the forward movement of speech. Voyce is an abstraction of my interlocutor. During our conversation, I listened for repetitions, interruptions, intrusions of the outside world, silences, tonalities, inflections, and affects. Then I asked Voyce to play Chopin's Walz op. 42, transcribed the piece's rhythmic ambiguity as well as my free-associations. The result is an experimental text, immersive in its focus on language and voice, sound and music, with variations in volume, pitch, and rhythm. It conflates the narrative, performative and conceptual dimensions of writing.

The Merri Creek Murders

As intimated in 'Otopos', the Merri Creek trail, which snakes through Melbourne's northern suburbs, is a popular retreat and recreational area. But it also attracts predators and there have been several attacks and murders in the area along the years. The incident in this sequence blends unrelated assaults perpetrated in recent years on women.

The epigraph is from Joan Fleming's *Songs of Less* (Cordite Books, 2022). 'In nearby bushes' makes reference to a haunting collection by Jamaican poet and fiction writer Kei Miller (Carcanet, 2019).

The phrase 'rushes bull and black' is taken from *The rhyme of the reddleman's daughter*, by James Simpson (The Hedgehog Poetry Press, 2019).

The italicised text in stanza 9 are reproduced verbatim from the Twisted History website available at *https://twistedhistory.net.au/2016/01/07/conspired-murder-and-suicide/*.

Fervour

The epigraph is from Carol Ann Duffy's *Rapture* (Picador, 2005).

A few words about the *Sacred Kingfisher festival*: For thousands of years the Merri Creek that courses through greater Melbourne was home to many different animals including the gorgeous blue kingfisher, who flew all the way from Queensland to nest there. But factories crept along the banks of the Merri and industrial waste mushroomed into the creek or onto a local rubbish tip. For the last 25 years environmentalists have celebrated the return of the Kingfisher to the Merri Creek. It continues to be a symbol of environmental hope.

'Then the wind of uncertainty blew at the peak of acquired knowledge' is a rephrasing of Raymond Queneau's *'then the wind of certainty will blow at the summit of acquired knowledge'*.

Rising is Melbourne's new winter arts festival. In 2021 it was to feature public art, performance, immersive experience and ceremony for ten days but was paused due to a third Covid lockdown.

I want to credit John Bailey's article 'Hidden Depths', published in *The Age* (May 22, 2021) from which I gleaned information about the festival as well as words from local Aboriginal languages. I respectfully use the name *yorro yorro*, meaning cascade, and the Woi Wurrung and Boon Wurring *iuk* meaning both eel and season.

In stanza 9, the italicised words refer to Immanuel Kant's *Critique of Judgement* (CJ, 5: 258).

'O deark dear K *amid the glow of day break'* is a twist on line 80 of Milton's *Samson Agonistes.*

ACKNOWLEDGEMENTS

Some of the poems in this triptych have previously appeared (sometimes in earlier, or bilingual, versions) in *Canto Planetario: Hermanda en la Tierra* (ed. Carlos Jarquin), *Live Encounters* (ed. Mark Ulysseas), *Meniscus* (eds. Gail Pittaway and Jen Webb), *Mot à Maux* (ed. Daniel Brochard), *Rabbit* (eds. Kent MacCarter, Micaela Sahhar and Jessica Wilkinson), *The Lockdown Poems* (ed. Rose Lucas), *Resilience: A celebration of poetry, fiction and essays from Mascara Literary Review* (ed. Michelle Seminara). My thanks to the editors of these journals and anthologies for their support and for providing fabulous platforms for poetry to be read.

Heartfelt thanks to Indran Amirthanayagam and Sara Cahill Marron for their stewardship at Beltway Editions; and to Jorge Ureta Sandoval for the book design. A warm mention to Eugen Bacon, Christine Hill, Linda Weste and Marion May Campbell for their encouragement.

EPILOGUE

There is much to savour and enjoy in this new, three-part collection by Dominique Hecq. I found myself absorbed in a layered sense of place, where a close attention to details of the natural/unnatural world and our shifting relationship to it comes to life off the page. This focus is interlaced with a commentary on language itself, how it inhabits the body and our breath. The repetition of the phrase 'unwrite the I from the poem' suggests the singular 'I' dissolves into the work, becoming 'us'. The self is both present and absent. Based in the UK, I am new to the complicated politics of land ownership, displacement, and the issues of the unceded Wurundjeri land but was introduced to these themes with delicacy and tenderness by Hecq's writing. There is no didacticism here. Merri Creek itself is a unifying through line in the collection, a place that becomes both real and fantastical. The pandemic hovers in the background, focussing the reader on the way nature begins to take over the city of Melbourne during this time period.

I was very moved by the shift in tone in the central section of the book, where the creek because a setting for a series of violent attacks on women. We as the reader become the onlooker who does not act, implicated in this darker world. Hecq's shifting of language registers from police reports to lyrical passages become acts of remembrance for the women involved. The more uplifting tone of the final section maintains Hecq's exquisite attention to sensory details, as a complicated love blossoms from the pages. 'Life is a chromatic fractal slipping into dusk' was a memorable image in this twilight world of animals and birds. Here is a musical poet capable of pyrotechnics, at ease with an extraordinary richness of forms and shapes on the page.

—Anne Caldwell, author of Karen, author of *Alice and the North*

Dominique Hecq

was born in the French-speaking part of Belgium. She now lives on unceded Wurundjeri land in Melbourne, Australia. Hecq writes in English and French. Her creative works comprise a novel, six collections of short stories and sixteen books and chapbooks of poetry. Her latest publications include *After Cage* (2nd ed., Liquid Amber Press, 2022), *Endgame with No Ending* (SurVision, 2023), a bilingual poetry sequence titled *Pistes de rêve/Songlines*, with photographs by Natia Zvhania (Transignum, 2024) and *Volte Face* (Liquid Amber Press, 2024).

Among other honours such as The Melbourne Fringe Festival Award for Outstanding Writing and Spoken Word Performance, The Woorilla Prize for Fiction, The New England Review Prize for Poetry, The Martha Richardson Medal for Poetry, and the inaugural AALITRA Prize for Literary Translation (Spanish to English), Dominique Hecq is a recipient of the International Best Poets Prize administered by the International Poetry Translation and Research Centre in conjunction with the International Academy of Arts and Letters and, more recently, the James Tate Poetry Prize.

BY THE SAME AUTHOR

Poetry

Volte Face (Liquid Amber Press, 2024).
Pistes de rêves (Editions Transignum, 2024).
Endgame with No Ending (SurVision Press, 2023).
After Cage: A Serial Composition in Word and Movement on Time and Silence, 2nd edition (Liquid Amber Press, 2022).
Kaosmos (Melbourne Poets Union, 2020).
Tracks: Autofictional Fragments of a Journey without Maps (Recent Work Press, 2020).
Kosmogonies (Encres Vives, 2019).
After Cage (Girls on Key Press, 2019).
With Béatrice Machet, Crypto (Flying Islands Press, 2018).
Hors Limites (L'Harmattan, 2018).
Hush: A Fugue (University of Western Australia, 2017).
Stretchmarks of Sun (Re.Press, 2014).
Out of Bounds (Re.Press, 2009).
Couchgrass (Papyrus Publishing, 2006).
Good Grief: and Other Frivolous Journeys into Spells, Songs and Elegies (Papyrus Publishing, 2002).
The Gaze of Silence (Sidewalk Collective, 1999).

Fiction

Smacked and Other Stories of Addiction (Spineless Wonders, 2022).
With Eugen Bacon, Speculate: A Collection of Microlit

(Meerkat Press, 2021).
Noisy Blood: Stories (Papyrus Publishing, 2004).
The Book of Elsa: A Novel (Papyrus Publishing, 2000).
Magic and Other Stories (Woorilla, 2000).
Mythfits: Four Uneasy Pieces (PenFolk Publishing, 1999).

Essay

Threading Through (Tacit Art, 2021).
With Julian Novitz, *Creative Writing with Critical Theory: Inhabitation* (Gylphi, 2018).
Towards a Poetics of Creative Writing. (Multilingual Matters, 2015).
The Creativity Market: Creative Writing in the 21st Century (Multilingual Matters, 2012).
With Russell Grigg and Craig Smith, *Female Sexuality: The Early Psychoanalytic Controversies* (Rebus Press, 1999).

OTOPOS

PRINTING WAS COMPLETED IN JULY 2024 FOR **Beltway Editions**